MADE
for the ICE

A Report on the Wreck of the
Hudson's Bay Company Ship *Baymaud*,
ex-Polarskibet *Maud*
(1917-1930)

James P. Delgado

Copyright © 1997
Vancouver Maritime Museum and Underwater Archaeological Society of British Columbia
1905 Ogden Avenue, Vancouver, B.C., Canada V6J 1A3

Canadian Cataloguing in Publication Data

Delgado, James P., 1958-

    Made for the Ice

Includes bibliographical references.
Copublished by: Vancouver Maritime Museum.
ISBN 0-9695010-4-8

1. Maud (Ship)
2. Underwater archaeology--Northwest Territories.
3. Shipwrecks--Northwest Territories.
I. Underwater Archaeological Society of British Columbia.
II. Vancouver Maritime Museum.
III. Title.
G530.M38D44 1997   910'.916327   C97-910366-5

Design and layout by Black Cat Graphics & Communications

Printed and bound in Canada by VCR Print Ltd.

Table of Contents

Acknowledgements

This project was undertaken by the Vancouver Maritime Museum in cooperation with the Underwater Archaeological Society of British Columbia. Funding for the project was provided by the Government of the Northwest Territories, Economic Development and Tourism. Logistical support was provided by the Hamlet of Cambridge Bay and the Cambridge Bay Volunteer Fire Department.

The project team wishes to extend its thanks to Marion Glawson, Regional Tourism Officer, and her immediate predecessor, Sheri Kemp-Kinear, as well as Glenda Parsons in the Economic Development and Tourism Office, Aimee Glawson at the Arctic Coast Visitor Centre, and Eddie Amagonalok and his family. We also thank Cambridge Bay Councillor Sydney Glawson, Marvin Sierks of the Cambridge Bay Volunteer Fire Department, Charles D. Arnold, Director, Prince of Wales Northern Heritage Centre, Margaret Bertulli, Arctic Archaeologist, Prince of Wales Northern Heritage Centre, Judith Hudson Beattie, Archivist, Hudson's Bay Company Archives, Tina Sangris of NWT Archives, and Brent Boddie, Ian McRae, Ann Goodhart, Leslie Paris, and Jennifer Stone.

Production of the project report was done by Black Cat Graphics and Communications.

Maud *at Nome, Alaska, June 1922. Glenbow Archives, Calgary, Loman Brothers Collection, NC-1-767(a).*

Introduction

The wreck of *Baymaud* lies near the Hamlet of Cambridge Bay (Iqaluktuuttiaq) on Victoria Island, in the Canadian Arctic archipelago. Situated just above the 69th parallel, Cambridge Bay is 350 kilometers north of the Arctic Circle. The wreck lies immediately off the old town site of Cambridge Bay in a section of the larger bay known as Carl's Bay.

A preliminary site inspection of the wreck of *Baymaud* was made by James Delgado, accompanied by local divers Brent Boddy and Ian McRae, on August 23, 1995. The wreck was documented and studied by James Delgado, Jacques Marc, Michael Paris, David Stone, and Robert Delgado between August 11-16, 1996. James Delgado was the principal investigator. The non-intrusive documentation of *Baymaud* was authorized by Northwest Territories

Archaeologists Permit #96-817, issued on June 17, 1996.

Field work was accomplished through 11 dives made by the team, most of them of an hour's duration, between August 11 and 16. The total number of diving person hours spent in the water was 53 hours. Using trilateration, and working from a template prepared from archival plans of the ship from Norway and the Hudson's Bay Company, a detailed, measured plan and starboard profile of the wreck was prepared. Site mapping was accomplished by Jacques Marc, David Stone, James Delgado, and Robert Delgado.

The wreck was videotaped, and a series of overall views, as well as individual features, were photographed with a 35 mm still camera. The videographer/photographer was Michael Paris.

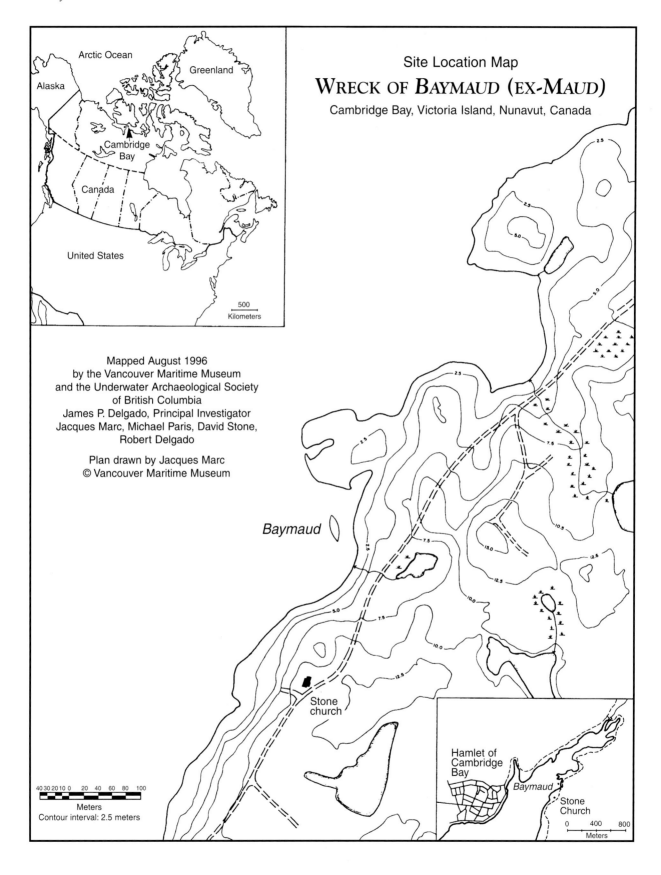

Site Location Map

WRECK OF BAYMAUD (EX-MAUD)

Cambridge Bay, Victoria Island, Nunavut, Canada

Arctic Ocean

Greenland

Alaska

Cambridge Bay

Canada

United States

500
Kilometers

Mapped August 1996
by the Vancouver Maritime Museum
and the Underwater Archaeological Society
of British Columbia
James P. Delgado, Principal Investigator
Jacques Marc, Michael Paris, David Stone,
Robert Delgado

Plan drawn by Jacques Marc
© Vancouver Maritime Museum

Baymaud

Stone
church

40 30 20 10 0   20   40   60   80   100

Meters
Contour interval: 2.5 meters

Hamlet of
Cambridge
Bay

Baymaud

Stone
Church

0   400   800
Meters

History of *Maud* and *Baymaud*

Maud was built for famous Norwegian polar explorer Roald Amundsen, leader of the first successful navigation of the Northwest Passage (1903-1905) in the sloop *Gjoa*. Following his Arctic exploits, Amundsen had raced and beat British explorer Robert F. Scott to the South Pole in 1911. The North Pole had been reached in 1909 by American explorers Robert E. Peary and Matthew Henson. Amundsen then set out to prove that a ship could be frozen into the Arctic ice and used as a floating scientific research station, perhaps even for years at a time. Nansen, in *Fram*, had frozen in and drifted with the ice to 84 degrees north between 1893-1896 in an attempt to reach the North Pole.

Amundsen planned to use *Fram* to reach the North Pole as early as 1913, primarily to demonstrate a vessel's survival and usability in a prolonged experiment, but the First World War intervened. It was not until 1916 that Amundsen was able to raise the necessary funds to begin serious planning. A new era of polar exploration, focusing on scientific observation, was beginning, and Amundsen's expedition was focused on science. Amundsen intended, as Nansen had done earlier, to get deliberately stuck in the ice and drift with it, taking meteorological, oceanographic and magnetic observations while enroute to the North Pole.

Amundsen's original intent to take *Fram* was thwarted by the ship's poor condition. He then decided to build a new vessel, modelled after *Fram* but with improvements. That vessel was *Maud*. The ship was launched at Asker, 30 kilometers southwest of Oslo on the shores of Oslo Fjord, on June 7, 1917. Amundsen named the ship for Queen Maud of Norway (1869-1938). Amundsen, christening *Maud* with a block of ice that he shattered against the bow,

proclaimed, "You are made for ice. You shall spend your best years in the ice and you shall do your work in the ice." *Maud's* construction cost was 900,000 kroner, or approximately $180,000 (Canadian) in 1917 dollars.

Amundsen sailed from Kristiana (Oslo) on June 24, 1918, heading north to Vardo, on Norway's Arctic coast. *Maud* sailed from Vardo on July 18. Amundsen's original plan, to sail into the Pacific and enter the Arctic through the Bering Strait, had been thwarted by the wartime danger of submarine attack. Instead, Amundsen decided to take the Northeast Passage, across the top of Russia and Siberia. Norwegian A.E. Nordenskjold had previously been the first to navigate the Northeast Passage, in the ship *Vega*, between 1878-1879. Amundsen's expedition would be the second. "I... decided to get into the Arctic by the shortest possible route. I therefore planned to skirt the coast of Norway from Oslo to Tromsoe. Thence I should make the Northeast Passage.... passing Cape Tscheluskin and rounding the New Siberian Islands, when I could strike into the same Arctic current which I would have made by proceeding first to Bering Strait." (Amundsen 1928:82)

Maud's launch, June 7, 1917. Vancouver Maritime Museum Collection.

After passing Cape Tscheluskin, the northernmost point in Asia, *Maud* encountered heavy ice. On September 17, Amundsen moored in the ice in the lee of two small islets. He named the anchorage Maudhavn (Maud Harbour). The ship remained there for a year. It was a difficult time for Amundsen; he fell down the ship's gangway and broke his shoulder, and then, several weeks later, was mauled by a polar bear. In December 1918, Amundsen nearly died from carbon monoxide poisoning while working in an unventilated observatory. Two of *Maud*'s sailors died while sledging for Russia and thence home. When *Maud* finally broke free of the ice, on September 12, 1919, the ship was able to navigate for only eleven days before freezing in for the winter at the mouth of the Kolyma River in Siberia. *Maud* was 500 miles short of the Bering Strait.

Maud was able to break out of the ice after several months. Amundsen, with his injuries and the loss of three of his crew (another man left in Siberia), decided to put into Nome, Alaska. When *Maud* arrived at Nome on July 27, 1920, he had completed the Northeast Passage, but was no closer to his original goal of drifting in the Arctic ice pack towards the North Pole. He did note, with wounded pride, that "When I anchored after sailing through the North East Passage, I succeeded in connecting it with my North West Passage of 1906, and thus for the first time completed a circumnavigation of the Arctic Ocean. In this day of records that might have some significance." (as quoted in Huntford 1987:104)

After a brief stop in Nome, Amundsen sailed again but was stopped by ice off Siberia's Cape Serdze Kamen for a third winter. When the ship finally broke free, on July 1, 1921, Amundsen turned back from the Arctic. The ship's propeller had been damaged by ice and other repairs were also needed. Amundsen sailed for Seattle, arriving on August 31. While *Maud* was repaired during the fall, winter, and spring of 1921-1922, Amundsen returned to Norway in January 1922 to regroup and seek additional funds

for the expedition. Important scientific observations, including detailed anthropological studies of the Chukchees of Siberia undertaken by the expedition's scientist, Dr. Harald Ulrik Sverdrup, during a seven-month hiatus on the land, had been completed, but after three years Amundsen had yet to achieve his original goal for the expedition.

Maud sailed from Seattle on June 3, 1922, and arrived at Nome on the 22nd, where Amundsen met the ship. He had changed his plans and brought two airplanes, one for short reconnaissance flights, the other for what he hoped would be the first transpolar flight. Amundsen left

Amundsen in the main cabin, circa 1919-1920. Vancouver Maritime Museum Collection.

Maud *frozen in for the winter, 1918-1919. Vancouver Maritime Museum Collection.*

Amundsen speaks from the forecastle deck at Nome, June 1922.
Glenbow Archives, Calgary, Loman Brothers Collection, NC-1-764(a).

with one plane for Wainwright, Alaska, to continue work on a transpolar flight. The aircraft left with *Maud* made three flights, the first in polar regions and the first from a ship as a base. The planned transpolar flight from Alaska did not take place and ultimately both airplanes were wrecked. It was not until 1925, on a separate expedition, that Amundsen would again attempt to fly to the pole.

Maud's fourth attempt to drift in the Arctic ice, sailing on July 13, 1925, under the command of Oscar Wisting, also ended in failure. Instead of drifting to the North Pole, *Maud* only reached 76 degrees, 51 minutes. Wisting turned back at the New Siberian Islands, arriving at Nome on August 22nd. There the ship was met by creditors. Amundsen's funds had run out and over-commitments by a business partner in the transpolar flight led him to file for bankruptcy. *Maud* managed to clear Nome but on arrival in Seattle on October 5th was again seized by creditors, who had outfitted the ship in 1922 and had never been paid. "Now the *Maud* will likely be sold", reported a waterfront journal, "and end her days as a coastwise or Puget Sound freighter." (*Railway and Marine News*, 1925:13) In all, $8,784.48 in liens were filed against the ship.

The Hudson's Bay Company purchased *Maud* at auction in Seattle in late December 1925 for $40,000 to supply H.B.C. outposts in the Western Arctic. The ship was renamed *Baymaud* and was towed to Vancouver between February 7-8, 1926, for refitting at the Burrard Shipbuilding and Drydock Company's North Vancouver yard. Ice had damaged the keel, skeg, and rudder post, and repairs to the engines were needed. Trials were held on English Bay, Vancouver, on May 25, 1926.

After minor adjustments, the ship was readied for the north. Loaded with supplies, principally lumber and case oil, *Baymaud* sailed from Vancouver on June 21, 1926, under the command of Captain Gus Foellmer of Vancouver. *Baymaud* called at Herschel Island and Baillie Island, and then into Coronation Gulf to land supplies at Bernard Harbour, Tree River, Kent Peninsula, and other outposts. The ship then sailed to the southwest coast of Victoria Island to establish a new H.B.C. post, Fort Harmon, and winter there. Arriving in September, the ship landed building materials, supplies, and two of the crew to erect the buildings. Captain Foellmer was concerned that the anchorage would not shelter *Baymaud* against the ice and sailed to Bernard Harbour to winter.

Baymaud broke out of Bernard Harbour and sailed through the ice of Coronation Gulf in late July 1927 for Kent Peninsula. The H.B.C. post at Kent River was dismantled and loaded into the ship between August 1-5, and *Baymaud* then sailed to Cambridge Bay, where a new H.B.C. post was to be established. *Baymaud* arrived at Cambridge Bay on August 7, and landed the building materials and supplies. The decision was made to leave the ship at Cambridge Bay, too, because the voyage under the H.B.C. flag had shown that the large ship, with her deep draft, "was not suitable for navigating the shoal waters of this section of the district." (Crisp 1955:47) Captain Foellmer left *Baymaud* behind, sailing from Cambridge Bay in the H.B.C. ship *Baychimo* on August 15. *Baymaud* was left "in safe harbour" and moored with wire rope to large boulders on shore, 90 fathoms of chain to the port anchor, and 65 fathoms of chain to the starboard anchor. (Logbook, August 9, 1927)

Baymaud was moored close to shore and used by the H.B.C. as a floating machine shop, warehouse and wireless station. Twice a day the wireless operator, W.G. Crisp, sent out regular weather reports through the R.C.C.S. Mackenzie network. These were "the first regular winter reports by radio from Canada's arctic coast." (Crisp 1955:47)

Frozen in at Cambridge Bay, 1930. Vancouver Maritime Museum Collection.

RCMP *St. Roch* visited Cambridge Bay for the first time in 1928. Then mate, soon to be skipper, Henry Larsen, later reminisced that "the *Bay Maud* was still anchored out in the bay and I found it sad to see Amundsen's fine ship as just another floating radio station." (Larsen 1967:45) The same year, Hugh Conn, General Inspector of the Hudson's Bay Company, reported that *Baymaud* "is anchored in a sheltered cove at the head of Cambridge Bay. The engines were taken down, well oiled and greased and the ship's gear carefully stored away as soon as possible after the ship was safely anchored. There is a slight leakage in the ship but the caretaker keeps a careful watch, day and night, so the water is never allowed to rise above the engine room floor. When it is decided again to commission the ship, she can be put in seagoing order in about two days." (Conn 1928:5)

Characteristics of *Maud* and *Baymaud*

Maud was built for Norwegian explorer Roald Amundsen at Christian Jensen's shipyard at Vollen, Asker, Norway, between 1916 and 1917. According to Oscar Wisting, who sailed with the ship as mate in 1918-1924 and who was *Maud's* captain after Amundsen in 1925, the ship incorporated some of *Fram's* fittings, including the masts, windlass, helm and propeller. (Wisting 1930:47) Amundsen claimed that the ship's basic design was his, and that the most important aspect was the shape of the hull. "This was to be the same shape substantially as the half of an egg cut through its length. In other words, the vessel's bottom would be rounded at every point, so that, when she should be caught in the grinding ice, there would be no surface on which the ice could take hold, while, on the contrary, the ice pressure would tend only to lift her to the surface. This shape also provided the greatest strength with the least surface." (Amundsen 1928:78)

*Maud under construction, 1917.
Vancouver Maritime Museum Collection.*

According to the ship's plans (Jensen 1917), *Maud* as built was 118 Norwegian feet long on deck, with a waterline length of 98 feet, 3 inches, an overall beam of 40 feet, a waterline beam of 34 feet, 9 inches, a depth of hold of 16 feet, and was registered at 380 gross tons. When registered by the Hudson's Bay Company in *Lloyds' Register* in 1926, the vessel was described as a three-masted auxiliary schooner, 106.8 English feet long, with a 40-foot beam, and a 15.3-foot depth of hold. The vessel was registered at 385 gross and 339 net tons.

The hull was heavily built of 12 x 12-inch floors, doubled and spaced at 13 inches. The frames gradually tapered to form 12 x 8-inch frames. The keel was oak, $13\frac{1}{2}$ x $10\frac{1}{2}$ inches, with a fir 12 x 12 false keel bolted to it. The keelson was formed with two $13\frac{1}{2}$ x $10\frac{1}{2}$-inch timbers, with two bilge keelsons or strakes to port and starboard, equally spaced in the hold and running fore and aft. These strakes were formed with two 7 x 7-inch timbers.

From the 'tween deck to the weather deck, two additional, equally spaced 7 x 7-inch strakes also gave the ship longitudinal strength.

At every second frame, both at the 'tween deck and the weather deck, diagonal struts, or "ice beams", were installed. These were formed by diagonal timbers and natural compass timber knees, iron fastened. The ice braces were located at every deck beam. The deck beams were 10 x 10-inch timbers, braced with wooden lodging knees fore and aft, and with 3-inch thick decking at the weather deck and $2\frac{1}{2}$-inch thick decking at the 'tween deck. The weather deck was supported by iron hanging knees through-bolted to the frames and a hold-beam shelf made from three 7 x 7-inch beams. The 'tween deck was supported by a hold beam shelf formed from three 7 x 7-inch timbers. The decks were also supported by 6 x 9-inch wooden stanchions on every beam, which were chamfered into the beam and braced with iron straps on their fore and aft faces. The hull was also braced with three solid thwartship bulwarks made with 3-inch thick, tongue-in-groove planks, with wooden braces iron bolted through them.

The outer hull planking was 4-inch oak, treenailed to the frames. A $2\frac{1}{2}$-inch ice sheathing was laid over the hull. It was oak from the keel to halfway to the deck, and greenheart from there to just above the waterline. The ice sheathing from above the waterline to the weather deck level was pitch pine. The ceiling planking was 4-inch oak. Amundsen noted that while building *Maud* "I was not satisfied to use the timbers available in Norway, so I imported specially fine timbers from Holland." (Amundsen 1928:79)

The ship carried three masts rigged as a barkentine. Each mast, with a topmast, carried a fore-and-aft rig with fixed gaffs and the sails on runners. These features avoided handling sails in icy conditions and also made it possible for a small crew to sail her. The foremast carried a single yard. *Maud* was also powered by a four-cylinder, 240-horsepower Bolinder semi-diesel engine that drove a single, two-bladed screw. The screw and the rudder were both retractable, an important feature for a vessel intended for use as a scientific research station frozen into drifting, shifting pack ice that could shear off rudders and propellers. Amundsen later said that *Maud*'s

> ... crowning glory was the engine room. Chief engineer Sundbeck managed to arrange a control centre down there, from which he controlled the whole ship. He could do the most unbelievable things just by pressing a button. A network of pipes was gathered here, so that he could have everything he needed - diesel oil, lubricating oil, etc. In my enthusiasm, when I first saw it all... I asked Sundbeck if he couldn't turn a tap, and give me an ale? "No," he answered faintly, "but you can always have a lager." (as quoted in Huntford 1987:167)

Bolinder engines were described in 1914 as "one of the comparatively few direct-reversible engines" then on the market. (*Motor Ship and Motor Boat* 1914:91) They engines were manufactured in Stockholm, Sweden. Bolinder engines were two-cycle (one impulse each revolution) "hot bulb" engines, which were described in 1922:

> .... a small quantity of fresh water (taken from the cylinder jacket) is injected into the cylinder at the same time as the fuel, with the object of reducing heavy knocking due to high compression pressures and temperatures. The water so introduced absorbs some of the heat in forming steam.... (Sothern 1922:39)

In later Bolinder engines, the water was replaced by compressed air, and then by a new injection device that did away with water and air that sprayed fuel directly on the piston. "With this new device it is possible to operate the engines at full load, keeping the ignition bulbs so cool that they are black; and it is also quite possible to run the engine indefinitely without load, the bulbs retaining their heat for any length of time." (Sothern 1922:267). *Maud* also carried a 15-h.p. Bolinder auxiliary engine "for the purpose of operating her anchor winch, cargo hoist, bilge pump and fire line, as well as auxiliary air pumps...." (French 1926)

Maud had a raised forecastle deck that partially protected the hand and power windlass. Immediately abaft the raised forecastle head were two enclosed water closets. Aft of them and the foremast was a single, 9-foot, 9-inch by 7-foot, 3-inch cargo hatch leading into the midships hold. A hand and power winch was located forward of the hatch and just abaft the foremast. Aft of the mainmast was a large deckhouse that housed the crew quarters in ten individual cabins, a galley, laboratory, and a central dining saloon. The cabin was made from 4 x 5-inch timbers, which were insulated with thick felt and then sheathed inside and out with $1\frac{1}{2}$-inch tongue-and-groove planking. The portholes were manufactured with double panes of thick glass to provide better insulation. The helm was located atop the forward end of the cabin. Aft of the cabin was a hatch and ladder leading into the engine room.

When purchased by the Hudson's Bay Company, *Maud* was modified. A new set of plans, dated February 15, 1926, were "traced and revised" by Vancouver naval architect Tom Halliday. (Halliday 1926) They show that an enclosed pilothouse, 5-foot, 7-inch by 9-foot, 3-inch, and 6-foot, 7-inch high, was built atop the cabin, and that the interior of the cabin was remodelled. The entry into the cabin, which had been from aft, was moved to the forward end, the two after cabins were extended across the aft bulkhead of the cabin, and the galley was relocated. These features are also present on a model of *Baymaud* made by the ship's carpenter, M. Walde, at Bernard Harbour during the winter of 1926.

Vessel Loss and Site Formation

According to wireless operator W.G. Crisp, "in 1930 the *Baymaud* developed a leak at her propeller shaft which could not be repaired without docking facilities. She sank at her moorings and became a complete wreck." (Crisp 1955:47) There is an unsubstantiated local oral tradition that the ship was "scuttled" by the Hudson's Bay Company. Company officials noted in June 1930 that "the *Baymaud* is leaking badly and we have already instructed our Western Arctic District Manager to try and arrange so that she can be put on the beach in such a way as to be useful for wireless plant and warehouse. She is of no further value to the Hudson's Bay Company." (French 1930) Photographs of the vessel taken at the time of her loss show that *Baymaud* settled by the bow and to port, with the starboard side and the stern rising above the water, along with the cabin and masts. The date of the ship's sinking appears to have been during the winter of 1930-1931. RCMP *St. Roch* radio operator John Duke photographed *Baymaud*

afloat at Cambridge Bay when *St. Roch* visited between August 15-16, 1930. When *St. Roch* returned to Cambridge Bay in September 1931, *Baymaud* had sunk. Duke took three photographs of the partially submerged wreck, including one of the nearly awash port bulwarks and deck. Duke's diary for September 11, 1931, notes that he "went

John Duke's photographs of the sunken Baymaud, *1930.*
Vancouver Maritime Museum, St. Roch *National Historic Site Collection.*

over to *Baymaud* – Amundsens boat used in 1918 Expedition to N. Pole. Unloading." (Duke 1930-1931)

H.B.C. records state that the ship was "dismantled" at the site between 1931 and 1932. One account notes that the Hudson's Bay Company's magazine (warehouse) at Cambridge Bay was "built from timbers removed from the *Baymaud* by L.A. Learmonth in 1933." (Historic Master Plan, Cambridge Bay 1994:4) This may have been confined to the deckhouse. According to local resident James Kavanna, who first visited the wreck in 1934, the masts were still upright and the decks were intact. Two photographs taken in 1935 show *Baymaud* in the ice, masts gone, the pilothouse removed, and the port bulwark broken away. A photograph published in the Vancouver *Sun* on October 6, 1937, shows a similar view. The Vancouver *Sun* article noted that the wreck was "gradually sinking deeper into the ice...." After then, Mr. Kavanna recalls, more of the wreck was pulled ashore and used as firewood. Another account stresses that "local people also scavenged material from the partially submerged wreck for homes." Mr. Kavanna specifically stated that a "mast" from the wreck was used to make the flagpole at the H.B.C.'s store. Henry Larsen, aboard RCMP *St. Roch*, noted that in September 1935 he sailed in to Cambridge Bay and "saw the Hudson's Bay flag at Cambridge Bay. It was flying from an old flagstaff which once had served as the foremast on the explorer Amundsen's ship *Maud*. The rest of the ship lay on her side near the shore, looking like a stranded whale." (Larsen 1967:100) In a 1947 interview, Larsen reported that when he arrived, oil was leaking from the wreck while "the Eskimos stripped the derelict apart." Because the oil was "destroying the fishing in the immediate area", Larsen "blew up the abandoned hull with dynamite." (*Marine Digest* 1947:2) Dynamite blasting might help explain the extensive damage to the ship's stern area, where the fuel tanks are located. With the cabin and aft deck blasted free, the tanks could be salvaged and drained. This would explain why not every fuel tank was located in the 1996 survey.

A photograph taken in July 1939 by Constable Derek Parkes, aboard RCMP *St. Roch*, then tied to the stern of the wreck of *Maud*, shows the exterior and interior of the stern, with the deck missing, lying higher above the surface and at a less steep angle than the wreck lies today. The exhaust, leading from the engine, protrudes from the water. The same view, again from the stern, is seen in a photograph dated as the summer of 1954 and published in the HBC magazine *The Beaver* in 1955. After this time, the wreck canted more to port and settled into deeper water, probably as a result of winter ice pushing the hull to port while it also settled deeper into the mud bottom of the bay.

St. Roch moored to the wreck of Baymaud, *July 1939. Photo Derek Parkes. Vancouver Maritime Museum,* St. Roch *National Historic Site Collection.*

Local residents note that the water surrounding the wreck's starboard hull freezes from the beach to the hull and down to the seabed. The interior of the hull and the port hull are at times ice-free, although in extreme winters the entire site is covered by ice floes. The movement of the ice, particularly with north winds or when the thick ice on the starboard side begins to shift and move offshore, surges and bangs against the hull. This is probably why the wreck has apparently been pushed forward (and down) and offshore, and the timbers and fastenings in the interior have sheared away on the starboard side, collapsing into the hold in the last 40 years.

Preservation/
Restoration Initiatives

Norwegian interest in the wreck of *Baymaud* has intensified over the past several years, but as early as 1935 the ship's wheel was returned to Norway after a Norwegian request for relics from *Maud*. The wheel had been removed from the wreck in 1931 and stored at Cambridge Bay until 1935.

The municipality of Asker purchased the wreck of *Baymaud* from the Hudson's Bay Company, which had until then never relinquished its rights to the ship, on November 28, 1990. The sale, for $1.00 (one dollar), was done so that Asker could raise funds to raise the wreck and return it to Norway for restoration. The restored ship would then be displayed as part of a new coastal cultural centre along with other boats and vessels in a "unique display of Norwegian craftsmanship and designing abilities at the turning of the century." The estimated cost in 1991 was 8.8 million Norwegian kroner to raise the wreck and transport it to Norway, and 11.2 million kroner to restore the ship to floating, operating condition. With a 15 percent contingency added, the total estimated cost was 23.0 million kroner. (Asker 1991)

Asker sent two representatives to Cambridge Bay in October 1990 to make a diving inspection of the wreck. The representatives, from the Norwegian maritime insurance and registration firm, Det Norsk Veritas, and from a Norwegian salvage firm, AMCON, videotaped the wreck. The Asker prospectus for the vessel's restoration (1991) noted that "the results from the diving inspection concludes that the wreck is possible to salvage and restore within reasonable cost... most of the deck is gone, as well as rigging and deck housing. The remains of the hull is however in a relatively good condition which will render a safe completion of the project.... In addition a number of original items have been discovered inside and in close vicinity of the wreck, which will contribute to the restoration." (Asker 1991:5) The prospectus went on to note that "the technical status of the wreck has been clearly reduced in the past 10 years, which is mainly due to ice breaking the deck area

down.... it is concluded that *Maud* should be salvaged within a short time. With a horizon of say, 10 years from now, the wreck will be far less interesting from a restoration point of view, despite the extremely good preservation conditions in Arctic waters." (Asker 1991:6)

The plan for salvage advanced in the Asker prospectus called for raising the ship "by establishing sufficient buoyancy in order to get the deck edge above water before pumping is commenced. Possible leakages will be sealed prior to start of salvage. This method is relatively cheap and comprises few unknown elements." (Asker 1991:9) The raised vessel, floating on her own keel, would then be towed eastwards through the Northwest Passage, assisted by an icebreaker. "*Maud* is considered to have sufficient residual strength" for towing on her own keel, the prospectus noted, "provided she is strengthened in some vital places. In addition, reserve buoyancy must be installed on board." (Asker 1991:10-11)

In February 1992, the Hamlet of Cambridge Bay offered the windlass (referred to in the correspondence as an "anchor winch") to the *Fram* Museum in Oslo, Norway, because the windlass had originally come from *Fram* before being requisitioned for *Maud*. *Fram* was then celebrating a 100-year birthday. The director of the *Fram* Museum requested an opinion from Asker. On April 2, 1992, the director of cultural affairs for Asker asserted Asker's ownership of the wreck, their opposition to removing any items from *Maud*, and offered a model of the ship and a selection of photographs from Amundsen's Northwest passage expedition to the Hamlet of Cambridge Bay to "ease the loss of the vessel itself" when *Maud* was taken back to Norway.

In 1993, Asker applied for and received a Canadian Cultural Properties Export permit to remove the wreck and take it to Norway. After this, Asker apparently transferred their ownership and rights to the vessel to the municipality of Tromso,

Norway, which would restore and display the ship there. Tromso is the home of the Roald Amundsen Institute, the Norwegian Polar Institute, and the Polar Museum. It was also *Maud*'s port of departure in 1918.

A recent (1996) Tromso prospectus rephrased the conclusions of the Asker (1991) prospectus, noting that "Det Norsk Veritas examined the wreck to see if it was possible to save the *Maud*, and the examination showed it is fully possible to save and restore the wreck.... the engines in the *Maud* can also be restored, according to experts." The Tromso prospectus notes that *Maud* "is in a terrible state of disrepair which is mainly due to ice that breaks the wreck down. Based on the development over the past years, the *Maud* has to be salvaged in a short time. In 5-10 years from this date, the wreck is considered to be so damaged that a restoration will be of little interest despite the good storage conditions in Arctic waters."

Baymaud's *windlass, August 1996. Photo Michael Paris. Vancouver Maritime Museum Collection.*

Site Description

The wreck of *Baymaud* lies 4.4 kilometers from the present Hamlet of Cambridge Bay, 60.8 meters immediately offshore and parallel to the beach. The wreck lies canted at a 20 degree angle away from the shore and the interior of the hull is exposed to the prevailing waves. The site is marked by an interpretive wayside exhibit. The beach is mixed rock and gravel, gradually sloping to a more abrupt drop-off. Silt covers the rock and gravel past this point; the wreck lies in a thick mud that is apparently as deep as a meter, perhaps more. The ocean bottom around the site is rock covered with loose silt that steeply drops to a narrow shelf at a depth of 6 to 7 meters.

The hull is held in place by the mud, which has mounded up against the port hull. The bottom of the hull is clear to the keel on the starboard side, and sufficiently clear to allow a diver to crawl along the keel along the entire length of the ship on the starboard side. The mounding of mud to port may be the result of the hull gradually sliding into deeper water on its port beam, pushing up the mud. There is also a meter-deep scour in the mud, running for approximately 5 meters in a straight line from the keel at the stern. A 625-gallon fuel oil tank lies beneath the hull on the bottom at the port stern quarter. This tank is visible on the hull in the 1939 Parkes photograph of the wreck and has subsequently fallen off the ship to the sea bottom. In 1995, the preliminary assessment indicated that the hull rested against this tank (Delgado 1995); closer examination beneath the hull in 1996 found that this is not the case.

The upper part of the starboard hull rises 2 meters above the surface, along with the starboard side of the weather deck at the bow and much of the windlass. Flat iron chainplates line the starboard hull and delineate the position of *Baymaud*'s three masts, which are no longer in place. The port side is intact to the main or weather deck level, which lies at a depth of 3-4 meters.

The bulwarks have completely broken on both beams, leaving only stubs of the bulwark stanchions. The hull at the stern is ice-damaged and gouged, the planks and frames broken away

to a level just below the original waterline, about a meter below the weather deck level. Timbers from the stern and the bow lie scattered along the bottom in the immediate vicinity of the wreck. Many of these timbers are broken and splintered planks and frames that are largely unidentifiable. However, a small grouping of frames from the stern lie on the bottom, roughly articulated and attached to each other, while a portion of the stem and a cant frame lie immediately off the bow.

The starboard hull of the wreck has lost ice sheathing in an area close to the bow. Sheathing is working loose on other parts of the hull and has separated at the curve of the bow and stern at the butt ends. It is splaying out from the hull, exposing the outer hull planking beneath it. The ice sheathing is also pulling away from the hull at the port stern quarter.

Starboard side, showing the mast and chainplates with deadeyes, August 1996. Photo Michael Paris. Vancouver Maritime Museum Collection.

The chainplates are flat strap iron through-bolted to the hull. The chainplates for the fore and main masts remain attached to the starboard hull, with the stubs of three of the mizzen chainplates also in place. The others are missing, although their positions are delineated by rust stains on the wood. The chainplates for the fore and mizzen masts were observed on the port hull. The chainplates, attached to the hull above the waterline, were shackled to single iron bars, 8 centimeters in diameter by 1.20 meters long, that passed through the bulwarks and terminated at the deadeyes. One of the round iron bars remains shackled to a main mast chainplate on the starboard side but the terminal end, with the deadeye, has been cut off. The foremast chainplates to port retain the iron bars on the first three plates and wooden deadeyes, 19 centimeters in diameter and possibly lignum vitae, are attached to the terminal ends. A fourth deadeye, attached to the iron bar, lies on the bottom next to the other foremast chainplates. There is no rigging passing through the deadeyes. However, a section of decayed hemp rigging is draped near the foremast chainplates and appears to be from the shrouds.

A section of a wooden mast rests at a steep angle against the foremast chainplates. It is also angled slightly toward the bow. The end closest to the surface is the keyed end that fits into the mast step. The mast, 37 centimeters in diameter, extends 5.05 meters to the bottom, disappearing into the mud. An iron mast band, with a saddle and goose neck for the gaff, remains attached to the mast, just above the mud. Despite its position next to the foremast chainplates, the placement of the mast band identifies it as the mizzenmast. The position of the mast, bottom

up and forward of its original, stepped position, seems to indicate that this mast was pulled free of the hull, partially salvaged, and dropped back onto the wreck.

Both the bow and stern are sheathed with flat iron bars (1.44 meters from the stem to port and starboard, 14 centimeters wide, 2 centimeters thick) that are fastened with iron drifts into the timbers. An iron shoe also protects the stem from the iron bars to the keel. There are fourteen bars at the bow. An additional bar from the bow, which was observed hanging from one fastening in August 1995 (Delgado 1995) has now detached and fallen. There are eight bars left attached to the stern; there were probably fifteen originally

Baymaud's bow (above) and stern, August 1996. Photos James Delgado.
Vancouver Maritime Museum Collection.

Baymaud's starboard side (above) and port side, August 1996.
Photos James Delgado. Vancouver Maritime Museum Collection.

but the bar sheathing at the stern is for the most part missing as a result of the grinding away of the stern by ice.

The weather, or main, deck is largely missing. The deck survives at the bow, although the planking is missing along the port side and the deck beams, which are exposed, are cracked and bent inwards. The deck terminates in the area of the foremast; the aperture for the mast remains in the decking, although it has broken here and the decking is falling away and into the ship. The level of the weather deck on the starboard side is above the surface of the water and is delineated by iron hanging knees that line the interior of the hull. Through-fastened to the hull with iron drifts, several of the knees are loose, and in some cases

the peened heads of the drifts have worn away or snapped off so the knees have pulled free of the hull at their lowest level. This may be the result of ice pushing against and lifting the tops of the knees. Two knees have fallen free of the hull on the starboard side and lie on the 'tween deck in close proximity to their original positions.

A small portion of the weather deck remains intact on the port side near the stern. It terminates 2 meters from the edge of the hull. Lying up against the stubs of the bulwarks and resting against the mizzen chainplates is the vertical steering engine from the ship's helm, with its standards, messenger wheel, guide pulleys, and scroll wheel visible. The vertical steering engine lies in a tangle of firebricks and tiles from the galley. The bricks

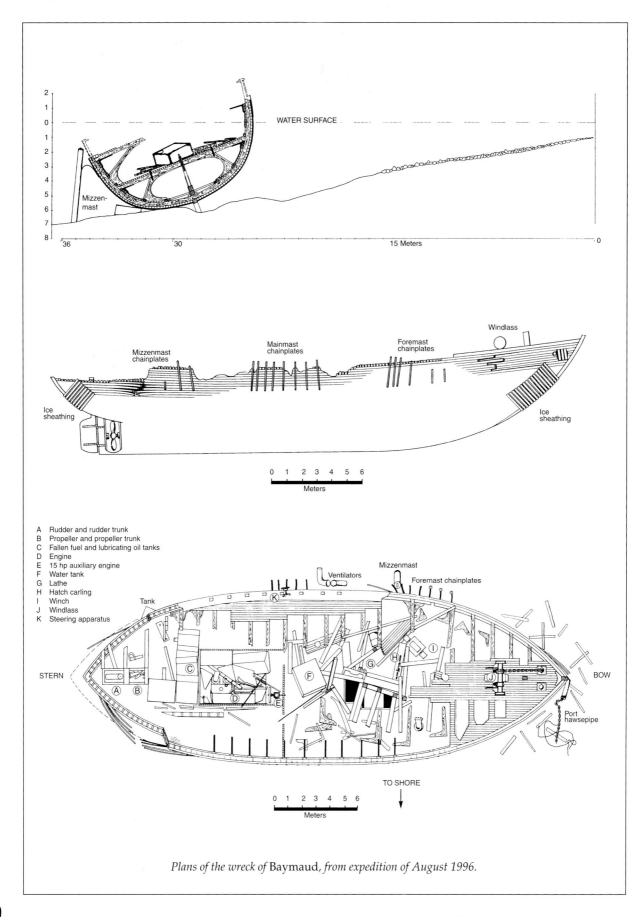

2
1
0 — — — WATER SURFACE — — —
1
2
3
4
5
6
Mizzen-
mast
7
8

36   30   15 Meters   0

Mizzenmast
chainplates

Mainmast
chainplates

Foremast
chainplates

Windlass

Ice
sheathing

Ice
sheathing

0 1 2 3 4 5 6
Meters

A   Rudder and rudder trunk
B   Propeller and propeller trunk
C   Fallen fuel and lubricating oil tanks
D   Engine
E   15 hp auxiliary engine
F   Water tank
G   Lathe
H   Hatch carling
I   Winch
J   Windlass
K   Steering apparatus

Tank

Ventilators

Mizzenmast

Foremast chainplates

STERN

BOW

Port
hawsepipe

TO SHORE

0 1 2 3 4 5 6
Meters

Plans of the wreck of Baymaud, *from expedition of August 1996.*

are of two distinctly different types. The first, a yellow brick, 13 centimeters by 22 centimeters, is stamped "CLAYBURN". The other, a red brick, 13 centimeters by 22 centimeters, is stamped "SOMENOS". The tiles, square glazed, 16 centimeters by 16 centimeters, are stamped "ALFRED RACOUT & CO., MAASTRICHT, HOLLAND." The galley was located in the immediate area, at the forward, port corner of the deckhouse. The removal of the deckhouse allowed these materials to slide along the deck as the hull rolled to port. No trace of the stove or other fittings from the galley were observed in this area.

The interior of the hull is divided by three athwartships bulkheads, at the forecastle, somewhat aft of the mainmast, and toward the stern. The aft two are linked by two longitudinal bulkheads to create a rectangular engine room compartment. The tongue-in-groove bulkheads, 17 centimeters thick, still retain traces of white paint.

The 15-h.p. auxiliary engine sits on a small deck immediately forward of the engine and against the thwartships bulkhead of the main hold. A shaft runs through; it was connected to geared shafts that ran to the deck winch or to other machinery. A length of detached shaft lies on the opposite side of the bulkhead and runs forward toward the winch.

Steering gear and loose firebricks from the collapsed galley lying on the waterway on the port side.

15-horsepower auxiliary engine. Photos Michael Paris. Vancouver Maritime Museum Collection.

Just aft of the engine room are four rectangular tanks, which lie toppled to port. These are identified in the ship's plans as 525-gallon capacity fuel oil tanks. A single half-round tank rests aft of them. It was one of a pair of 625-gallon capacity "oil" tanks located on the weather deck behind the cabin.

The engine room is largely obscured under four triangular tanks. These were 340- and 310-gallon capacity tanks for lubricating oil and coal oil. The ship's plans show them suspended from the ceiling and side bulkheads, which left adequate head room over the engine. Two of the tanks are badly ruptured at the seams. The ship's engine remains in place, though largely hidden under a fallen tank. There is substantial damage to the four "hot bulbs". One seems to be intact but another has disappeared completely and two more are partially broken off. The lower parts of the engine were not observed as access is obstructed. The engine is identifiable as a four-cylinder Bolinders semi-diesel and matches contemporary photographs of this type of engine.

Plans show that the power plant extended below the 'tween deck level into the hold and that access to it was possible through a hatch aft of the cabin.

The exhaust pipe survives in pieces. The upper portion, visible in the 1939 photograph of the wreck, lies to port. The lower section is broken from the engine and upended. Observation confirms that it trunked up and aft as shown on the ship's plans of 1917; a different configuration on the 1926 plan reflected drawing style rather than a modification. There is also an array of thin pipes which run to various points in the engine room from a shelf in the starboard aft corner. These are probably remnants of Sundbeck's controls.

The machinery in the engine room is covered with thick, loose orange corrosion which easily brushes off. The metal has cracked in numerous places and appears brittle.

Historical accounts stress that the ship sank because of a leak where the single propeller shaft passed through the hull. The shaft could not be traced inside the hull as there is no safe access. However, the shaft is visible where the two-bladed iron or steel propeller is mounted. The propeller is fitted into a trunk, with grooved iron tracks fore and aft that allowed the crew to pull the propeller up and free of the ice. The rudder, which is canted slightly to port, also rests inside a rectangular trunk. A thick steel loop at the top of the rudder allowed the crew to also hoist the rudder free of the ice.

Inside the hull, the lower or 'tween deck has survived intact. It is buried by collapsed and broken deck beams, decking, ice braces, lodging knees, and the hatch coaming and carlings. The hatch carling, with the ship's tonnage information, was found

collapsed in the hull. Part of the carved inscription is visible and reads "NE 292 71/100 TONS MQWS" RE 29— TO—". One end is splintered and broken away.

Three iron knees that have fallen off the starboard hull lie on the 'tween deck. The 'tween deck may be beginning to separate from the starboard hull; a 3-centimeter gap was noted between the deck and the hull that does not appear to be a construction feature. Open hatches in the 'tween deck open into the hold, which was not penetrated. There is no clear or unobstructed access to the hold without removing timbers.

View of the rudder, looking down the trunk.

Diver Jacques Marc hovering over the midships area of the wreck above fallen deck beams and ice braces. Photos Michael Paris. Vancouver Maritime Museum Collection.

*Interior of the forecastle. Photo Michael Paris.
Vancouver Maritime Museum Collection.*

Inside the hull, in the area of the main hatch, a riveted iron fresh water tank, identified in the ship's plans as an 875-gallon capacity tank, lies close to its original position amidships, just forward of the engine room's forward bulkhead. The tank has shifted forward and is angled to port. Forward of it, a lathe lies on its side, to port. The lathe is probably an original item from the ship's career as it is listed in *Maud's* 1925 sale inventory. No manufacturer's plate or other identifying marks were observed on the lathe.

The ship's winch was observed lying on its side, buried by fallen timbers. While no manufacturing information was observed, from its characteristics it appears to be a "Bolinders-Cyclops winch," which was a self-contained type of motor winch driven by a single-cylinder Bolinders oil engine. This type of winch was described in 1914: "the motor drives the winch through a double purchase spur gearing, consisting of a pinion keyed on the crank-shaft, gearing to a spurwheel. This spurwheel is itself keyed on to an intermediate

shaft, gearing into a spurwheel on a barrel shaft. The pinion on the intermediate shaft is fitted with a friction clutch of the expanding ring type, and the winch is so arranged that only one lever is required for operating." (*Motor Ship and Motor Boat*:149)

The bow, with its largely intact weather deck, was entered and examined. A tongue-in-groove bulkhead of 17-centimeter thickness separates the forecastle from the main hold; this bulkhead has collapsed from roughly the midships line and to the port side, allowing access into the forecastle. As mentioned previously, the weather deck planking is missing on the port side, allowing access into the forecastle from above.

The 'tween deck is intact inside the forecastle, with open hatches leading into the chain locker, which is divided by a longitudinal bulkhead into port and starboard boxes for the chain. There is a small amount of chain inside the port box, which is the source of a strand of chain that runs up to the windlass and then out of the hole in the bow that once mounted the port hawse pipe. An intermediate deck directly above the chain locker has collapsed and fallen aft.

A geared shaft is attached to the underside of the remaining weather deck. It apparently ran forward from the winch to a gearing mechanism on this intermediate deck and thence up to the windlass. What appears to be the remains of this gearing mechanism lies in the hold, on the starboard side, just forward of the forecastle bulkhead. The remains of an oil-fired water heater lies in the forecastle area.

The forecastle's 'tween deck is littered with loose planking and a conglomeration of coiled and heaped hemp line. Two blocks, a single and a triple sheave block, lie atop the line at the forward end of the bow, close to the stem. A large-diameter single steel block also lies inside the bow, on the starboard side and directly on the 'tween deck. Two masses of what appears to be a vegetable matter or fabric, perhaps decayed carpet, lie on the starboard side of the forecastle. A collapsed wooden stave barrel, with decaying matter inside of it, lies against the aft bulkhead on the starboard side of the forecastle.

Examination of the bow at the forward end of the forecastle shows three compass timber wooden crutches, at approximate 45 degree angles, reinforcing the stem. The crutches are working free and the iron fastenings are pulling away from the timber. The cant frames are loose and a gap is opening between the frames, planking and the stem. This may be evidence that the bow, because of the hole caused when the port hawse pipe tore free, is beginning to split.

The windlass is bolted to the weather deck at the bow and its starboard end rises above the water. The windlass is intact but is missing the hand-power levers. While not covered with corrosion, the windlass iron has cracked in numerous places.

The windlass' manufacturing information is cast on the crosshead and reads:

PUSNES ST. & MEK VERSTAD

ARENDAL, NORGE

NO. 11 35

The Pusnes workshop remains in business in Arendal, Norway.

The anchor cable, stud link chain measuring 13 by 19 centimeters, comes up from the forecastle, passes over the port-side cable lifter, through the hawse, and out of the hull to the bottom. The hawse pipe has pulled free of the hull and slid down the chain to rest on the starboard side of the stem. The chain runs out 2.90 meters from the hawse and terminates in the mud. When surveyed for the Hudson's Bay Company in Vancouver in April 1926, the ship carried 105 fathoms of 1½-inch stud link cable. (Scott 1926) The area of the port hawse has broken and splintered, tearing a roughly 1.30 by 1.0 meter hole in the bow immediately above the waterline. This was the only hole through the hull observed in 1996. The port hawse is intact, with the hawse pipe inside it, but the cast lip at the end of the pipe has sheared off. The ice sheathing and outer hull planking surrounding it has torn off to the stem post, exposing the frames. The stem is broken and is pulling away in this area, and the cant frames are loose surrounding it. The debris lying on the bottom in front of the bow includes the top end of the stem that formerly ran up to the forecastle deck and at least one broken cant frame. Three meters off the starboard bow is a tangle of wire rigging and an iron band from either the bowsprit or a topmast.

An anchor believed to be *Baymaud*'s was observed by local divers and was photographed in 1992 (Vralstad 1996) in deeper water to the port side of the ship. This anchor was not observed in 1996, but only a casual search was made for it as the priority was documentation of the wreck. If it is *Baymaud's*, then it should be marked "7189 Ingley, N.H. 7189 L'pool and London," and weigh 16 cwts. (Scott 1926) The anchor and stud link cable were identified in 1926 as "originally [from] Larsen's polarship FRAM...." (Holmrod 1926)

Bow of Baymaud, *showing the port anchor cable and hawsepipe.*
Photo Michael Paris. Vancouver Maritime Museum Collection.

Conclusions

Site Formation Process and Current Condition

The wreck of *Baymaud* demonstrates a site formation process in which the floating vessel became a shipwreck through an initially slow, gradual process that is now accelerating. A relatively rich pictorial record documents the condition of the wreck's exposed portions, beginning right after *Baymaud* sank until the current day.

Photographs of the wreck taken in September 1931 apparently show the ship not long after her sinking, as the masts are rigged and the ship's burgee, or pennant, is flying from the mainmast. The vessel settled by the bow and to port when it sank. A gouge in the mud bottom running in a straight line off the keel was made either when the ship sank and moved forward along the shallow bottom, or was gouged as the wreck slowly slid forward as a result of ice pressure and movement after sinking. The gouge is probably a result of the sinking process, as a comparison of the exposed starboard hull of the wreck with the 1931 photographs shows that the ship remains in the same position today. It has now settled deeper into the mud bottom and the water to an estimated depth of an additional 1.5 to 1.8 meters, or approximately 5 feet. This is demonstrated by a

1931 view of the port bow, taken from the port bulwark abaft the foremast, which shows that the water level is just at the caprail and that the deck is half awash, with the port waterway in about a meter of water. The depth of the port waterway in 1996 is approximately 2.5 meters at this same location. This is not entirely due to additional rolling of the hull to port, as 1931 and 1996 photographs show that the starboard hull has settled to approximately the same level.

The transformation of *Baymaud* from a sunken ship to shipwreck was at first a human process of salvage. The masts were removed from the wreck, as local tradition and the relocated bottom end of the mizzenmast clearly indicate. Examination of the flagpole at the old H.B.C. store (now the Northern Stores warehouse) did not conclusively identify it as a *Baymaud* mast or spar, although its dimensions and age would argue for a confirmation of oral tradition. The removal of other materials from the wreck is mentioned and may have been largely confined to the dismantling of the superstructure and some decking. The steering apparatus, firebricks, and tiles on the port side of the deck in the area of the cabin may suggest that they were directly deposited there in a more or less straight line by falling from their original position, higher on the deck and in the cabin and pilothouse. A 1935 photograph of the wreck shows the steering apparatus attached to the deck of the cabin, exposed to the weather. When the cabin was blasted by Larsen, the apparatus apparently fell into the water and caught on the submerged hull.

The 1939 photograph of the wreck, taken from the deck of RCMP *St. Roch*, which was moored to the half-sunk *Baymaud*, shows that the aft deck is missing. The deck forward also may have been missing by then. However, the survival of

View into interior of stern area, as seen from St. Roch, *July 1939. Photo Derek Parkes. Vancouver Maritime Museum,* St. Roch *National Historic Site Collection.*

the weather deck at the bow might suggest that the deck from midships forward survived the blasting and salvage of the aft super-structure and then slowly succumbed to ice and surge. The deck continues to work free of the wreck in 1996 as the exposed ends of the planks move with the surge and continue to pull free of the surviving deck beams.

Stern view showing ice damage, August 1996. The hull is worn down to below the waterline. Note the flat iron ice sheathing protruding above the outer hull planking, and the rudder. Photo Michael Paris. Vancouver Maritime Museum Collection.

Ice is the greatest force involved in the breaking down of the wreck after Larsen's 1935 blasting. Local informants, photographs, and video (including a 1992 underwater video of an ice dive) show that thick ice forms around the wreck. The movement of this ice as it forms and breaks up in annually recurring cycles has resulted in the wearing away of the stern to its level just below the original waterline and the disintegration of the deck. The collapse of decking, deck beams, and ice braces into the hold is a clear indication of downward thrust by the ice. The higher position of the stern after sinking, and its greater exposure to ice, has assisted in the greatest amount of damage occurring there.

The wreck of *Baymaud* may appear to be relatively stable, but it is not. The rate of deterioration, largely as a result of ice and surge damage, appears to be accelerating. Timbers were observed moving in the relatively light surge caused by both wind and boat and seaplane wakes, and deck timber continues to wash ashore from the wreck. The hull is opening at the bow and the 'tween deck is separating from the starboard hull. The weight of the surviving deck and windlass at the bow may be causing directional stress on the weakened bow. This, as well as the splitting of the bow along the stempost, will probably lead to the collapse of the surviving decking and the opening of the stem

down to the keel. The 'tween deck, now weighted with collapsed decking, timbers, and machinery from the weather deck, and no longer protected from ice by the weather deck, will gradually break down. When this happens, the hull will split at or around the keel and the port side will collapse into deeper water. The starboard hull, now visible above the water, would probably also collapse and be completely submerged.

One striking observation is the discrepancy between the 1996 observations and those reported as being from the 1990 Norwegian diving inspection report. The hull, which was thought in 1990 to survive to the main deck level, has broken down to the original waterline at the stern. The hole in the bow and the separation of the bow at the stem also were not noted. The 1990 report forecast a five to ten year period during which the wreck would be capable of recovery by raising it intact. That period is rapidly ending. We roughly estimate – with the caveat that it is done without the benefit of timber stress tests or other analysis – that a two to five year period is all that remains before a major hull collapse above the former waterline.

The 1990 Norwegian prospectus called for pumping out the ship and floating *Baymaud* on her own keel. While the hull's condition appears fair and probably watertight below the waterline, it is very poor above the waterline. It is our opinion that the wreck is incapable of floating on her own keel if pumped out and raised. Were the ship to be raised, it would require raising on slings, or in pieces, and need to be placed on a barge for transportation. Prior to such a recovery, more complete documentation of the wreck would be required, including significant clean up and removal of collapsed structural members, decking, and machinery, as well as an assessment of any remaining fuel or other petroleum products in the ship's tanks, some of which remain in the hold and could not be reached by divers until the deck above was cleared. Careful bracing of the hull and replacement of some of the missing weather deck beams would also be needed to insure a safe lift. Regardless of what approach is taken, it is clear that without some level of intervention the wreck of *Baymaud* is an archaeological site in transition. It should not be viewed as a "stable" site that will always be visible to shore-based tourists.

Significance

There are five polar exploration vessels preserved as museum ships in the world. They are *Gjoa* and *Fram* in Norway, *Discovery* in England, *St. Roch* in Canada, and *Hero* in the United States. A number of other vessels, either built for or used in polar exploration, were lost in Arctic or Antarctic waters. Only the wreck of *Baymaud* is precisely known and accessible for research, possible recovery and display.

Built as *Maud* and wrecked as *Baymaud*, the wreck at Cambridge Bay is an internationally significant cultural resource and archaeological site of particular interest to both Norway and Canada. The wrecked vessel, still substantially intact and a preservable entity with archaeological integrity, is significant to Norway because of her strong association with explorer Roald Amundsen and his last seagoing expedition. The *Maud* expedition of 1918-1925, while ultimately unsuccessful in reaching the North Pole, was of particular scientific significance and was one of the last great Arctic voyages of exploration.

Built for Amundsen, with his direct involvement in her design, *Maud* embodies a Norwegian

shipbuilding tradition that created some of the most successful and famous polar exploration vessels of the 19th and 20th centuries. *Maud* specifically represents a refinement of her predecessor, *Fram*, in that *Maud* is an improvement on *Fram*'s design, while at the same time recycling some of *Fram*'s fittings and equipment. These remain aboard the wreck to this day.

Maud also embodies features in her construction that, like those in *Fram*, represent international experience in ship handling and survival in polar regions. Much of this experience was acquired by Great Britain, which led international efforts to probe the Arctic throughout the first three-quarters of the 19th century.

European exploration of the Arctic began in the 16th century and blossomed between the mid-18th century and the mid-19th century. In the 19th century the Antarctic was also probed and its waters also charted. The conditions, particularly the problems of ships being frozen into pack ice, resulted in unique stresses to wooden hulls that resulted in the loss of vessels. Vessels specifically designed for "polar" voyages were not built until the late 19th century. Until then, existing vessels were modified for use.

The British Admiralty emphasized the use of former bomb vessels – heavily-built floating platforms for seagoing mortars – as polar exploration vessels. Six bomb vessels were converted to this use, beginning with HMS *Furnace* in 1741. It was followed by HMS *Carcass* and HMS *Racehorse* in 1773-1775 and then by HMS *Fury* in 1821. The last two bombs converted to polar exploration were the famous HMS *Erebus* and HMS *Terror*, used in Ross' Antarctic expeditions of 1836 and 1839 and finally in the ill-fated Franklin expedition of 1845-1848. Bomb vessels were used repeatedly because they were "peculiarly well-suited to Arctic voyages," with "squarish midship section[s], bluff bow and strong construction of the hull (to withstand the firing of the mortars)...." that provided "the right combination of strength and internal capacity...." (Ware 1994:94)

Specific modifications for the ice included reinforcing the bows and bracing the hull. In 1773, the Navy Board specifications for modifying *Carcass* and *Racehorse* stipulated "that the bottoms of said sloops may be doubled; their bows fortified by breasthooks and sleepers, and additional riders added in the space between the bomb bed." (as quoted in Ware 1994:99) *Erebus* and *Terror* were modified for polar exploration in 1836. They were reinforced and were equipped with a detachable propeller and rudder, both of which could be lifted clear of the ice. The propeller was raised by a special hoisting mechanism through a trunk. (Ware 1994:100) Admiralty draughts of the two also show that an extra layer of planking was added to form an ice sheathing. The bottom of the hull was sheathed with 1$\frac{1}{2}$-inch thick "Canada Elm," while the sides were sheathed with elm and oak that thickened from 2 to 8 inches at their widest (at the wale). The ceiling planking was reinforced with two thicknesses of 1$\frac{1}{2}$-inch African iroko wood running diagonally across each other. The main deck was strengthened with 3-inch thick fir planks run diagonally across the original oak deck. (as shown in Ware 1994:102)

The British experience with ships in polar regions, as well as the Scandinavian experience with ice, seems to have influenced the design and construction of *Fram* and *Maud*. Similarly, the design of *Maud* very definitely influenced the design of the last great wooden vessel built for Arctic work, Canada's Royal Canadian Mounted Police auxiliary schooner *St. Roch*.

Maud's form and details were copied by Vancouver architect Tom Halliday in 1928 when he designed *St. Roch*. Halliday had supervised the refit of *Maud* and traced and revised plans of the Norwegian vessel in February 1926. In November 1927, he was handed the task of designing an Arctic schooner for the Mounties, working with a set of general specifications provided by Charles Druguid, naval constructor for the Department of the Marine in Ottawa. *Maud*'s hull and fittings had survived years of heavy ice during Amundsen's expedition, so Halliday copied the ship's lines and several construction details while planning *St.Roch*.

Norwegian-born RCMP Sergeant Henry A. Larsen, who watched the ship's construction and later commanded *St. Roch*, specifically noted that "the rudder itself was made of Australian gumwood, and was fitted in such a way that it could be raised up on deck through a specially constructed rudder-well similar to the one on Amundsen's *Maud*." (Larsen 1967:38) Among other previously-unknown shared characteristics were most significantly the lines – the round, egg-shaped hull. Other common features, which may or may not have been "borrowed" by Halliday, included the additional ironwood planks that formed an extra layer of "ice sheathing" on the hull, thick beams to brace the hold against the crushing pressure of ice floes, and a large cabin aft.

The significance of the ship to both Norway and Canada reaches beyond the hull's characteristics or how they offer more detailed information on the design and construction of polar exploration vessels. *Baymaud*'s significance is also linked to a shared history that saw the ship engaged in two careers under separate flags. As *Maud*, the ship explored the Arctic coast of Europe and Asia and played a significant role in advancing Arctic exploration from "discovery" to scientific observation. As *Baymaud*, the ship played a role in the transformation of Canada's Arctic coast from an isolated region into an active centre for trade connected to the world by radio. It is this shared history, as well as the ship's voyages to Russia, Siberia, and the United States, that confers an international significance to the wreck of *Baymaud*.

Recommendations

The story of *Maud* and *Baymaud* is little known outside of Norway and Cambridge Bay, where the wreck rests 66 years after sinking. Any work that adds to the public's understanding of the ship's characteristics, career and condition as an Arctic shipwreck should be encouraged. The ship's preservation also needs to be considered.

There are four options for the preservation of the wreck. They are:

1) Maintain the status quo;

2) Stabilize the ship as a wreck in Cambridge Bay;

3) Recover the ship for restoration as a floating or dry-land display;

4) Recover portions of the ship for dry-land display.

If the status quo is maintained, the vessel will continue to break up and will eventually be completely submerged. Once submerged, the wreck will be relatively stable as an archaeological site. There is no marine borer activity because of the cold, brackish water of the site. As a broken up wreck beneath the ice during the winter, the ship would not be subjected to the stresses of ice moving against the hull. The wreck would only be accessible to visitors through diving or through a museum/visitor centre on land that displayed drawings, photographs or underwater video.

If this option is pursued, then expanded interpretation of the ship's history and the submerged wreck at the Arctic Coast Visitor Centre, or the proposed Cambridge Bay Museum, is strongly encouraged. Consideration should also be given to a mylar or plastic encapsulated map or plan of the site, with prominent features identified, to guide divers around the wreck and explain what they are seeing. This last recommendation should also be considered as part of the next option. If diving on the wreck is encouraged, as it should be, then divers should be required to check in at the visitor centre to receive the map and to be formally informed that there is a policy of no active disturbance and no collecting from the wreck. Penetration of the wreck should be discouraged because of the likelihood of tangling and collapse.

Stabilizing the wreck at Cambridge Bay is an active intervention that would require periodic maintenance of the ship in an effort to keep the hull from splitting and submerging. Bracing the starboard side of the hull, probably by tying it to the port hull with replacement deck beams, and bracing the bow and its surviving decking, perhaps with diagonal ties, should be considered. The wreck would then remain visible to shore-based visitors as well as divers. If this option is pursued, interpretation of the submerged portions of the site is strongly encouraged, again with a museum/visitor centre display on land that utilized drawings, photographs or underwater video. Additional interpretation of the wreck at the site is also encouraged. An expanded wayside exhibit, with photographs of the ship before and immediately after it sank, as well as a drawing that orients the shore-based visitor to what portion of the ship is visible, would be essential. As well, the immediate environment on the shore around the wreck requires a clean-up for a better experience for the average tourist.

If recovery of the wreck is undertaken, this archaeological survey should not be considered sufficient for salvage assessment. A detailed assessment of the vessel's condition for salvage should be accomplished. The discrepancies between the 1990 and 1996 surveys of the wreck should at the minimum require a reworking of the Norwegian salvage and restoration prospectus to reflect the current condition of the wreck and any changes in the method of recovery and restoration, as well as increased costs. Analysis of the vessel's salvage potential should include timber and metal sample analysis and the active participation of a conservator with underwater and Arctic experience. The wreck is also an underwater archaeological site and a plan for detailed archaeological participation in the recovery of the vessel, including further site mapping and analysis, should be completed as part of the overall planning process.

Under no circumstances should salvage be undertaken until all planning is complete and funding is in hand. Despite continuing ice stress and damage, the wreck is in better condition after 66 years underwater than if the hull were raised and allowed to rapidly dry in a non-Arctic environment. Before Canada agrees to the repatriation of the wreck, it should be assured that adequate planning and funding is in place.

In the event of recovery and restoration of the ship in Norway, we strongly encourage a cultural exchange between Canada and Norway that results in a shared, international interpretation of *Maud*. If the wreck leaves Cambridge Bay, interpretation could include a model of the ship, in addition to photographs and video. Norwegian interests in Asker at one time offered a model of the ship as *Maud*. This, along with the display of the ship's carpenter's model of the ship as *Baymaud*, would be ideal centrepieces of a Cambridge Bay display. Items or fittings from the wreck that are not used in the restoration could be considered for conservation and display in Cambridge Bay. At the same time, interpretation of the ship's career as *Baymaud* in Norway would be enhanced with photographs of *Baymaud* from Canadian archival sources, and perhaps with a model of the ship as *Baymaud*.

Other artifacts from the ship may reside in Canadian collections. The Vancouver Maritime Museum, for example, holds a "fireless cooker" (catalog number M 973.485.32) that was used aboard the ship during Amundsen's expedition. The cooker was removed by *Baymaud*'s H.B.C. captain and was ultimately donated for museum display by his widow. Another artifact in the Museum's collection is a deadeye from *Baymaud* (catalog number M 984-33) removed by a RCAF flight lieutenant in the spring/summer of 1949.

The final option, of recovering pieces of the wreck for dry-land display, should only be considered as an option if the wreck breaks up and completely submerges, and then only if the recovery of portions of the wreck proceeds as an archaeological project, with conservation and adequate funding assured. It could also be a solution that Solomon would have applied to the dilemma of preserving and interpreting a ship desired by Norwegian interests in Tromso and by local interests in Cambridge Bay, as conserved portions of the wreck could be displayed in both localities.

Before any consideration of recovery is undertaken, we stress that further research on the wreck is recommended. Rather than focusing on potential recovery, this research should assess the ship's design and construction as part of a larger project that places *Maud* in context with earlier polar exploration vessels. It should particularly assess the transition in design and construction between *Fram, Maud,* and *St. Roch*, which now appear to be lineal design descendants. Detailed architectural assessment of the three ships should take place. This would include the preparation of a lines drawing for *Maud* based on underwater survey and partial excavation to allow access to the holds, as well as the removal of hull planking to assess framing details for comparison with *Fram* and *St. Roch*.

In conclusion, the wreck of *Baymaud* is a significant cultural resource that deserves a careful, considered program of research, interpretation and preservation. The status quo, which appears to range from neglect to well-intentioned but inadequate plans for recovery and restoration, is not working. International dialogue and cooperation, sharing of knowledge, and a mutual commitment to the wreck's preservation and interpretation is essential.

Sources Cited

Amundsen, Roald

1921   *Nordostpassagen: Maudfaeren Langs Asiens Kyst 1918-1920, H.U. Sverdrups Ophold Blandt Tsjuktsjerne, Godfred Hansens Depotekspedition, 1919-1920.* Gyldendalske Boghandle, Kristiana.

Amundsen, Roald

1928   *My Life as an Explorer.* Doubleday, Doran and Company, Garden City, New York.

Baymaud

1926-27   Chief Officer's Log, RG3/6A/1, Hudson's Bay Company Archives, Provincial Archives of Manitoba, Winnipeg.

Bonnycastle, R.H.G.

1935   "Address to the League of Norsemen on Occasion of Presenting Steering Wheel [of *Maud*]," E.154/24, Hudson's Bay Company Archives, Provincial Archives of Manitoba, Winnipeg.

Conn, Hugh

1928   Report, A/102/1047, folio 131, Hudson's Bay Company Archives, Provincial Archives of Manitoba, Winnipeg.

Crisp, W.G.

1955   "Amundsen's *Maud*", *The Beaver*, Summer, pp. 43-47.

Delgado, James P.

1992   *Dauntless St. Roch: The Mounties' Arctic Schooner.* Horsdal and Schubart, Victoria.

Delgado, James P.

1995   Report on a Preliminary Assessment of the HBC Ship *Baymaud*, ex-Polarskibet *Maud* (1917-1930). Manuscript, Prince of Wales Northern Heritage Centre, Yellowknife, NWT

Delgado, James P.

1997   "Arctic Ghost", *Equinox*, No. 92, April/May, pp. 56-61.

Duke, John

1930-31   Diary, August 3, 1930-November 24, 1931. Photocopied manuscript, *St. Roch* National Historic Site Collection, Vancouver Maritime Museum.

French, C.H.

1926   Letter to Fur Trade Commissioner, Hudson's Bay Company, Vancouver, June 17, *Baymaud* correspondence, 1925-1931, A.105/8, Hudson's Bay Company Archives, Provincial Archives of Manitoba, Winnipeg.

French, C.H.

1930   Letter to the Governor and Committee, Hudson's Bay Company, Winnipeg, June 3, *Baymaud* correspondence, 1925-1931, A.105/8, Hudson's Bay Company Archives, Provincial Archives of Manitoba, Winnipeg.

Halliday, T.

1926   General Arrangement and Capacity Plan of Auxiliary Arctic Schooner "Maud," Drawing No. 794A, February 15, HBCA Map Collection, A.109/40 Sheet 5 (N13114), Hudson's Bay Company Archives, Provincial Archives of Manitoba, Winnipeg.

Holmrod, Rode

1926   Cable to Hudson's Bay Company, Oslo, May 15, *Baymaud* correspondence, 1925-1931, A.105/8, Hudson's Bay Company Archives, Provincial Archives of Manitoba, Winnipeg.

Huntford, Roland, ed.

1987   *The Amundsen Photographs.* The Atlantic Monthly Press, New York.

Jensen, Christian

1916   "Polarskip for Herr Kapt. Roald Amundsen," Ship's Plan, Profile and Sailplan, November, HBCA Map Collection, A.105/8, Sheet 1 (N13112), Hudson's Bay Company Archives, Provincial Archives of Manitoba, Winnipeg.

Jensen, Christian

1917   "Polarskip for Herr Kapt. Roald Amundsen," Ship's Plan, Hull Profile and Deck Plan, January, HBCA Map Collection, A.105/8, Sheet 2 (N13113), Hudson's Bay Company Archives, Provincial Archives of Manitoba, Winnipeg.

Larsen, Henry A.
1967   *The Big Ship*. McClelland and Stewart, Toronto.

Marine Digest
1947   "Historical MS *St. Roch* Visits Seattle", Vol. 25, p. 55, August 23.

Motor Ship and Motor Boat, **Staff of**
1914   *The Marine Oil Engine Handbook*. Temple Press, London.

Sannes, Tor Borch
1989   *Fram*. Norsk Maritimt Forlag A.S, Oslo.

Scott, A.
1926   Letter to C.H. French, Hudson's Bay Company, Vancouver, April 20. *Baymaud* correspondence, 1925-1931, A.105/8, Hudson's Bay Company Archives, Provincial Archives of Manitoba, Winnipeg.

Sothern, J.W.M.
1922   *Notes and Sketches on Marine Diesel Engines: A Manual of Marine Oil Engine Practice*. James Munro & Co. Limited, Glasgow.

Tombs, George
1991   "The Strange Fate of Amundsen's Ship 'Maud'", *Above and Beyond*, Summer, pp. 59-62.

Underhill, Harold A.
1946   *Masting and Rigging: The Clipper Ship and Ocean Carrier*. Brown, Son and Ferguson, Glasgow.

Vralstad, Hans
1996   Pa jakt etter Roald Amundsen i Nordvestpassasjen, in *Norsk Sjofartsmuseum Arsber etning, 1995*. Norsk Sjofartsmuseum, Oslo.

Ware, Chris
1994   *The Bomb Vessel: Shore Bombardment Ships of the Age of Sail*. Conway Maritime Press, London.

Wisting, Oscar
1930   *16 Ar Med Roald Amundsen: Fra Pol til Pol*. Gyldendal Norsk Forlag, Oslo.